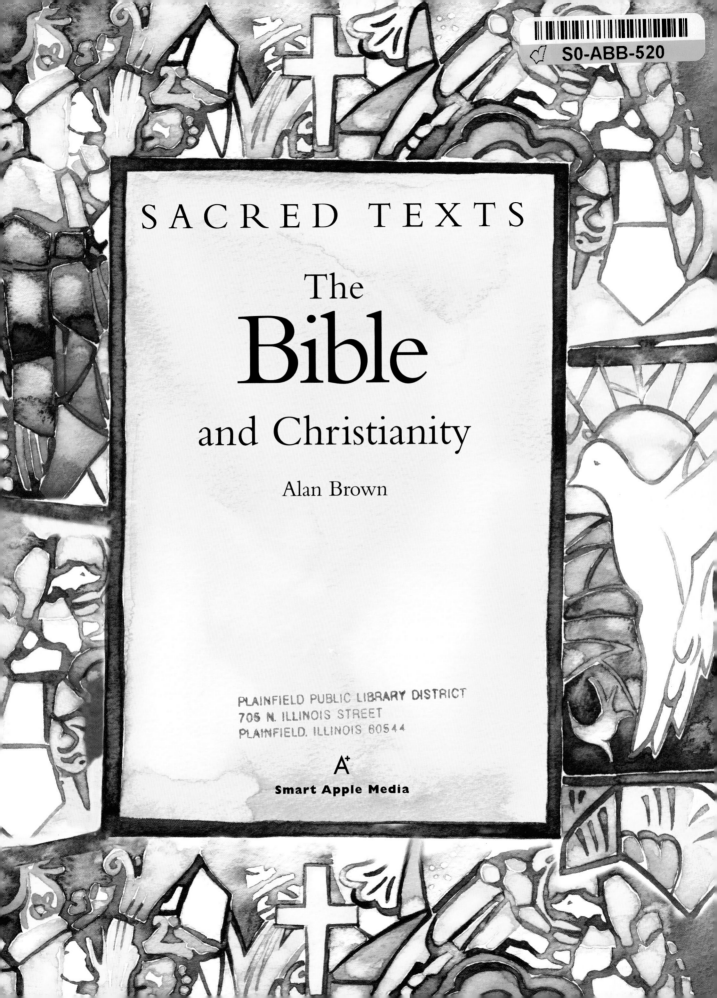

SACRED TEXTS

The
Bible
and Christianity

Alan Brown

A⁺
Smart Apple Media

Evans Brothers Limited
2A Portman Mansions
Chiltern St.
London W1U 6NR

First published 2003

Printed in Hong Kong by Wing King Tong Co. Ltd

Editors: Nicola Barber, Louise John
Designer: Simon Borrough
Illustrations: Tracy Fennell, Allied Artists
Production: Jenny Mulvanny
Consultant: Paul Uden, Diocese of Westminster

Picture acknowledgements:
theartarchive: p6 (Cathedral of Monreale Sicily /
Dagli Orti), p13 (The Art Archive / S Maria della
Salute Venice / Dagli Orti), p15 top (The Art Archive
/ Pinacoteca Nazionale di Siena / Dagli Orti), p18
(National Gallery of Art Washington / Album / Joseph
Martin), p20 (Montemaria Abbey Burgusio Bolzano
Italy / Dagli Orti), p21 (Dagli Orti), p23 (British
Library)
The Bridgeman Art Library: p8 (British Museum,
London), p9 (British Library, London), p12 (Stapleton
Collection), p15 bottom (Biblioteca Reale, Turin,
Italy), p16 (Laura James)
Circa Photo Library: p11 top & bottom (Barrie
Searle), p17, p19 (John Smith), p26 (John Smith)
Corbis: p7
Hutchison Picture Library: p22 (Michael Macintyre),
p24 top (J Wright), p24 bottom (Polfoto, Denmark),
p27 bottom (Sarah Errington)
Life File: p25 (Sergei Verein)
Trip: p27 top (H Rogers)

Published in the United States by
Smart Apple Media, 1980 Lookout Drive
North Mankato, Minnesota 56003

Library of Congress Cataloging-in-Publication Data

Brown, Alan.
The Bible and Christianity / by Alan Brown.
p. cm. — (Sacred texts)
Summary: Explains how the Old and New Testaments
came to be part of the Bible used by Christians and
discusses some of the important messages found in the
holy scriptures.
ISBN 1-58340-243-8
1. Bible—Juvenile literature. [1. Bible.] I. Title. II.
Sacred texts (Mankato, Minn.)

BS539.B76 2003
220—dc21   2003041645

First Edition
9 8 7 6 5 4 3 2 1

In this book, dates are written using B.C.E., which means "before the common era," and C.E., which means "of the common era." These abbreviations replace B.C. ("before Christ") and A.D. (*anno domini*, "in the year of the Lord"), which are based on the Christian calendar.

The quotations in this book are taken from the New English Bible, published by The Bible Societies, in association with OUP and CUP, 1961.

Contents

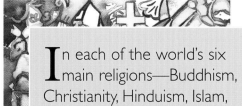

In each of the world's six main religions—Buddhism, Christianity, Hinduism, Islam, Judaism, and Sikhism—sacred texts play an important part. They teach people how to practice their faith and guide them through their lives. Wherever these books are read or studied, they are treated with great care and respect because they are so precious.

Introduction

The Christian Bible

The Bible is the most important book for Christians. It is split into two sections, the Old Testament and the New Testament. The Old Testament contains the account of the relationship between God and the Israelites, his chosen people. The New Testament tells Christians that God came to Earth as Jesus of Nazareth. Christians believe that Jesus is their savior, for he showed them how much God loved the world and the people in it.

How Christianity began

Jesus was born in Bethlehem, in Israel, in about 6 B.C.E. He was born into a Jewish family and was brought up in the Jewish faith. When he was in his 30s, he began to teach about God's love for the world. Jesus gathered 12 followers, called disciples, around him and with their help challenged the religious leaders of his time. He was put to death by crucifixion by the Roman government in about 31 or 32 C.E. Christians believe that after three days Jesus rose from the dead and appeared to his followers, before finally being taken into heaven.

In many Orthodox churches, the figure of Jesus is painted on the ceiling. This represents Jesus as judge.

The Holy Book

The first section of the Christian Bible, the Old Testament, is almost the same as the Jewish Bible. However, Christians understand the Old Testament in a very different way from Jews (see page 10). The second section, the New Testament, is the story of Jesus and the importance of his life for Christians. It contains four Gospels, each giving an account of the life of Jesus. It also contains letters written to early Christians explaining Jesus's life and encouraging them to be faithful.

A young Catholic girl reads the Bible.

Christianity today

Today, there are about two billion Christians, living in every country of the world. About half of them are members of the Roman Catholic Church. The others belong to more than 22,000 other Christian churches. The word "church" is used in three different ways. It can describe a local group of Christians, or it can be used as the name of the building in which Christians worship. It can also mean a whole group of Christians.

"God loved the world so much that He gave His only Son, that everyone who has faith in Him may not die but have eternal life."

(JOHN 3: 16)

What is the Bible?

The early Christians called the Old Testament "scripture." The words "Old" and "New" Testament only began to be used about 200 years after Jesus's death. "Testament" means "promise," and the Christian Bible is the story of the promises made by God. Christians also believe that the New Testament helps them to understand the Old Testament.

The Old Testament

The Old Testament is made up of 39 different parts, called books. These books contain stories from everyday life, as well as amazing adventures, terrifying battles, dreams, and visions. At first, the events recounted in the Old Testament were handed down by word of mouth. People wrote them down over a period of about 1,000 years, between about 1100 B.C.E. and 200 B.C.E. Christians believe that the Old

Early Bibles contained hand-painted illustrations.

Testament foretells of the coming of their savior, Jesus. They use the stories in the Old Testament to show that everything points to him.

The New Testament

The New Testament contains 27 books. It was probably written between 50 C.E. and 130 C.E. The earliest writings came from Paul, who travelled around the Mediterranean writing letters to new churches (see pages 20-21). These are called the Epistles, meaning "letters." The four Gospels were written between about 65 C.E. and 95 C.E. They are accounts of Jesus's life, death, and resurrection. They are like biographies, telling the life story of Jesus. There are also two other books in the Bible: the Acts of the Apostles, the story of the very early church, and the Revelation of St. John, the last book in the Bible.

When the Bible came together

It took more than 300 years for the early Christians to decide on the final number of books to make up their Bible. They finally agreed at the Council of Carthage, in 397 C.E. Some churches, such as the Orthodox and Roman Catholic churches, still include more books in their Bible than others. The Roman Catholic Church, for example, has a special section called the Apocrypha included in its Bible. The word "Apocrypha" means "hidden" or "obscure," for only very educated people were able to make sense of it.

"It is this same disciple who attests what has here been written. It is in fact he who wrote it, and we know his testimony is true. There is much else that Jesus did. If it were all to be recorded in detail, I suppose the whole world could not hold the books that would be written."

(JOHN 21: 24-25)

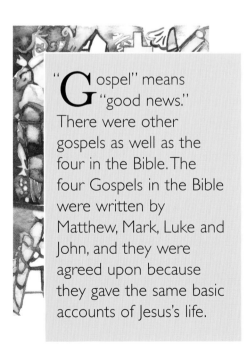

"Gospel" means "good news." There were other gospels as well as the four in the Bible. The four Gospels in the Bible were written by Matthew, Mark, Luke and John, and they were agreed upon because they gave the same basic accounts of Jesus's life.

Jesus surrounded by a man, a lion, an ox, and an eagle, the symbols of the four writers of the Gospels: Matthew, Mark, Luke, and John.

The Old Testament

How Christians use the Old Testament

Jesus was a Jew. He knew the Jewish scriptures well, and most of his teachings were familiar to the Jews to whom he spoke. When later followers wrote about the importance of Jesus's life, they wanted to show that the Jewish scriptures pointed directly to Jesus, their savior.

"Hear, O Israel, the Lord is our God, one Lord, and you must love the Lord your God with all your heart and soul and strength." (DEUTERONOMY 6: 4-5)

Different understandings

For Jews, the text of their scripture is not the only basis of their faith. In Judaism, the teachings of the rabbis (religious teachers) down through the centuries are very important. These teachings make sure that Jews continue to study and understand their scriptures in the light of the modern world. Christians read their Old Testament in view of what they believe about Jesus and the teachings of the New Testament. So the same story or same event has a different meaning for Jews and Christians.

The Old Testament was first written in Hebrew. The New Testament was first written in Greek. The whole Bible was later translated into Latin, and today, Bibles can be found written in many different languages.

The Jewish scriptures are processed around the synagogue (Jewish house of prayer) during a service.

Is the Old Testament true?

Some Christians believe that every word in the Old Testament is literally and historically true. Others believe that the stories and events have something to say about God, about Israel, and about human beings. They believe that the stories, handed down over centuries by word of mouth, say very important things about the love of God. However, the stories may not have happened exactly as they are written down.

What is in the Old Testament?

The Old Testament contains a variety of books written by different authors over many years. There are law books and history books. The Book of Psalms is rich in poetry, and the Book of Proverbs is full of wise advice. There are books in which prophets such as Hosea and Isaiah tell Israel to give up evil and turn back to God. Christians believe that these prophets tell of the coming of Jesus, who is the Messiah, the anointed king of the Jews. The Old Testament says that God created the world, put people in it, and watched over their triumphs and their mistakes. Of these people, the

The Jewish Bible (Torah) is handwritten with great love and care by a specially trained man called a sofer.

Israelites were chosen to be special to God, to follow and be obedient to His will. The story of Israel is the story of the Old Testament. It is a story full of both tragedy and happiness. Christians believe the story of Israel is the story of God loving a people. Christians are the "New Israel" because they also accept Jesus as God's son.

Stories and teaching

Christians believe that many of the events in the Old Testament are more fully understood if you believe in Jesus. They think that the stories of great figures such as Abraham, Moses, and David have real meaning only when the story of Jesus is known and accepted.

Abraham and Isaac

Abraham was an old man who was asked by God to sacrifice his beloved son, Isaac. With a heavy heart, Abraham and his son travelled to the place of sacrifice. Abraham tied Isaac up and prepared to kill him. At the last moment, an angel called out, telling him to stop. Abraham had shown that he was obedient to God and would give God anything—even his son. Abraham spotted a ram caught in a bush and sacrificed that instead. Christians read into this story Jesus's obedience to his father, God. They believe it shows the strength of God's love—His son, Jesus, was sacrificed to save the world from evil.

Moses the lawgiver

God appeared to Moses as he was tending sheep in the desert. He told Moses that he was to bring the Israelites out of Egypt to freedom. After 10 terrible plagues afflicted the Egyptians, Moses led the Israelites out of Egypt. Throughout the next 40 years, Moses was given the law that became the foundation for both Judaism and Christianity. The best-known section of this law is the Ten Commandments (see page 13). Christians believe that Jesus was the new Moses, leading the people of God into the Kingdom of Heaven.

God parted the Red Sea to allow Moses and the Israelites to escape from Egypt and reach the desert.

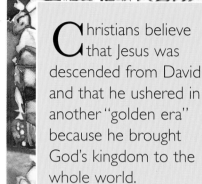

A painting of David killing Goliath, by the famous Italian painter Tiziano Vercellio Titian (1487–1576).

David

David was a shepherd boy and harp player from Bethlehem who killed the giant Goliath with a stone from his shepherd's sling. The prophet Samuel anointed him as God's chosen king of Israel, and David made Jerusalem the home of the Jews 1,000 years before the birth of Jesus. His reign was a golden period in Israel's history, and his story captured the imagination of Jews and Christians alike.

Isaiah

Christians believe that Isaiah, who lived more than 700 years before Jesus, prophesied Jesus's coming. Isaiah talked about the Lord God tending his flock like a shepherd and God's servant being despised, humbled, and having to suffer for carrying the sins and evil of the people. Christians believe Isaiah was speaking of Jesus and how he would be treated by his enemies.

"I am the Lord your God. You shall have no other god
You shall make no images of anything in heaven or earth
You shall not swear using God's name
You shall keep the Sabbath day holy
Honor your father and mother
Do not commit murder
Do not commit adultery
Do not steal
Do not lie
Do not want other people's possessions."

(EXODUS 20: 1-17)

13

The New Testament

The beginnings

The story of Jesus is at the heart of the New Testament. All the writers of the New Testament wanted the people who read their words to believe that Jesus was the Son of God, who was born to reunite people with God. They wrote for different readers, some Jews, others non-Jews (Gentiles). They also occasionally told the same stories in different ways. There are two stories of Jesus's birth in the Gospels, one in the Gospel of Luke and one in the Gospel of Matthew.

Luke

Luke tells how Mary, Jesus's mother, was visited by an angel who told her she had been chosen by God to have a child. The child would be called Jesus. Mary is at the heart of the story of Jesus's birth. Luke was keen to show how important women were in the early church and in the life of Jesus. He was also interested in poor and ordinary people. The baby, Jesus, was born among the animals and laid in a manger. The news of Jesus's birth was first given by the angels to the lowly shepherds in the fields, and they were the first to visit Jesus and pay tribute to him.

"The angel said, 'Do not be afraid; I have good news for you; there is great joy coming to the whole people. Today in the city of David a deliverer has been born to you—the Messiah, the Lord. And this is your sign: you will find a baby wrapped in his swaddling clothes in a manger."

(LUKE 2: 10-12)

The Magi (wise men) visit the baby Jesus in Bethlehem.

The festival of Christmas was not celebrated until 300 years after the death of Jesus. When Emperor Constantine became the first Christian Roman emperor in the early fourth century C.E., he decided that the Roman festival of Saturnalia should be replaced with a festival of Christ's birth. The crib scene came even later. It was not until the 13th century that St. Francis of Assisi is believed to have created the first crib scene.

Matthew

Matthew tells of Jesus's birth in Bethlehem, but in his story, Jesus's father, Joseph, is very important. Joseph was told of Jesus's birth in a dream. Dreams were one of the ways God was believed to speak to people. Magi, or wise men, came from the East to find the newborn king. These men were not Jews. Matthew wanted to show that Jesus is for Jews and non-Jews. The Magi brought gifts: gold for a king, frankincense for worship, and myrrh, a spice used to anoint the dead.

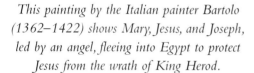

This painting by the Italian painter Bartolo (1362–1422) shows Mary, Jesus, and Joseph, led by an angel, fleeing into Egypt to protect Jesus from the wrath of King Herod.

Mission and message

The Bible tells how Jesus began his teaching when he was baptized by John the Baptist in the river Jordan. John was Jesus's cousin. He had already started to spread the word of God. But when John saw Jesus come for baptism, to be washed clean of his sins, he recognized Jesus as a person greater than himself. At the baptism, a voice came from heaven, saying, "Behold, my Son, in whom I am well pleased." Jesus selected 12 disciples (followers) to join him in his teaching. He taught for three years in Galilee, in the north of Israel, and around Jerusalem, in the south.

Jesus performs a miracle and gives sight to a blind person. Jesus often healed deaf and blind people as a sign that those who followed him would see and hear what he taught.

Jesus's teachings

Jesus taught that the time had come for God's kingdom to rule over the world. He asked people to listen to what he said and watch what he did. If they could understand, they would believe in him, accept God's will, and carry out His wishes. With understanding, they would find peace.

Parables

Jesus taught by using parables. A parable can be remembered as a good story, but it also has a deeper meaning. Jesus taught that the power and love of God is within people, and that this love will grow if people do God's will. This parable is in two of the Gospels, Matthew and Luke:

"If anyone has 100 sheep and loses one of them, surely he will leave the 99 in safety and go to look for the one missing sheep. When he has found it, he will bring it home on his shoulders and ask others to join in the celebration, for they have found what was lost. So, Jesus said, 'God is happy when even one person comes back to God.'"

"The kingdom of god is like a mustard seed, which a man took and sowed in his field. As a seed, mustard is smaller than any other; but when it has grown it is bigger than any garden-plant; it becomes a tree, big enough for birds to come and roost among its branches." (MATTHEW 13: 31-32)

Miracles

Jesus also used miracles to teach. The Gospels show that these miracles were signs of the power of God. There are many stories of Jesus healing people, but Jesus offended the Jewish religious leaders because he not only healed people, he also forgave their sins. The leaders believed that only God could forgive sins, and Jesus's claim was considered blasphemy.

There is only one miracle that is in all four Gospels. It is the "Feeding of the Five Thousand." In this miracle, Jesus feeds 5,000 followers with only five loaves and two small fishes. When everyone has had their fill, there are still 12 baskets of food left over.

In another miracle, Jesus turned water to wine at a wedding in Cana, Galilee.

Jesus's death and resurrection

For Christians, Jesus himself is of great importance, as well as what he taught. Christians believe that Jesus's teaching is summed up in the events of the last week of his life, and it is those events that make him so special. The Gospels tell that, after being pursued by the authorities for spreading the word of God against their will, Jesus was arrested, tried, then killed on a cross before rising from the dead three days later (called the Resurrection).

The Last Supper

Shortly before he died, Jesus ate a last meal with his disciples. When they broke bread and drank wine together, Jesus said, "Do this in remembrance of me." He told the disciples that one of them would betray him to the authorities and that Peter, his chief disciple, would deny knowing him three times before the cock crowed at daybreak. Then he left and went to pray. Judas, one of the disciples, notified the soldiers and led them to where Jesus was praying. He had been paid 30 pieces of silver to betray Jesus. Judas identified Jesus by giving him a welcoming kiss, and the soldiers arrested Jesus immediately.

The Last Supper, *painted by Spanish artist Salvador Dali in 1955, shows Jesus sharing his final meal with his disciples.*

The Crucifixion

The Bible tells of Jesus's trial before the Jewish court and high priest, and then before the Roman governor, Pontius Pilate. While Jesus was on trial, Peter was asked three times if he was a friend of Jesus. Each time he denied knowing who Jesus was. The governor handed Jesus over to be flogged and crucified. Jesus carried his cross to Golgotha, the Place of the Skull, where he was crucified between two criminals. His hands and feet were nailed to the cross. When he died, his body was taken down from the cross, wrapped in a sheet, and placed in a grave cut out of rock. A heavy stone was rolled across the opening.

The Resurrection

The Crucifixion took place on Friday afternoon, before the festival of Passover began. After the festival, on Sunday, Mary, the mother of Jesus, and Mary Magdalene, one of Jesus's followers, went to the tomb. They found the stone rolled back. The tomb was empty, except for an angel who told them that Jesus had risen from the dead, as he said he would. The angel told the women and the disciples to go to Galilee, where they would see Jesus.

The paschal candle is a powerful symbol of Jesus's life and death. It is lit at Easter time, when Christians celebrate the Crucifixion and Resurrection of Jesus.

"Thomas, one of the disciples, said, 'Unless I see the mark of the nails on his hands, unless I put my finger into the place where the nails were, and my hand into his side, I will not believe. . . .' A week later . . . Jesus came and stood among them, saying, 'Peace be with you!' Then he said to Thomas, 'Reach your hand here and put it into my side. Be unbelieving no longer, but believe.' Thomas said, 'My Lord and my God!'"

(JOHN 20: 24–29)

Paul the letter writer

The first writings about the life of Jesus are in the Epistles of Paul. These Epistles include letters to the people of Galatia, Thessalonia, Corinthia, and Rome. Paul was not alive at the same time as Jesus, but he became a great Christian leader, taking the message of Jesus to Greece, Asia Minor, and Rome. He died in Rome in about 62 C.E. Paul and the writers of other letters tell modern Christians a lot about what happened after the death of Jesus.

Paul's conversion

Paul was a tent maker from Tarsus, in modern-day Turkey, where he was known as Saul. He trained as a Jewish scholar and tells his readers that he watched and helped in the persecution of Jesus's followers by the Jewish authorities. One day, on the way to persecute Christians in Damascus, he saw a vision of Jesus. Jesus said to him, "Saul, Saul, why do you persecute me?" Paul was struck blind until a follower of Jesus healed him a few days later. He changed his name to Paul to start his new life and spent several years thinking about what had happened, and what he should do next.

An early picture of the apostle Paul. It is not known what he looked like, though he was described as "small, with a rather large nose, bald headed, and strongly built."

Paul's writing

Paul began to write to small groups of Christians in a number of towns and cities. He believed that Jesus's message was not just for Jews but for everyone, and he managed to persuade Jesus's disciples that he was right. Paul encouraged Christians to be strong in times of hardship. He showed how Jesus's rising from the dead had changed the world.

The importance of Paul

There are probably nine of Paul's letters in the New Testament (although scholars do not agree on the exact number). Paul was important because he wrote to Christians who had never seen Jesus. At that time there were no books about Jesus, although there may have been collections of Jesus's sayings. Paul changed the way that Jesus's followers taught. He tells his readers that he argued "face to face" with Peter about whether Gentiles (non-Jews) should be able to become Christians without becoming Jews first. Paul travelled continually, spreading the Christian faith, until he was taken to Rome and probably executed.

"Christ is like a single body which has many parts; it is still one body even though it is made up of different parts. In the same way, all of us, whether Jews or Gentiles, whether slaves or free, have been baptized into one body by the same Spirit."

(1 CORINTHIANS 12: 12–13)

Ephesus, where Paul taught, was a busy city with a great, thriving theater. The remains of the theater can still be seen there today.

Daily Life and Worship

Important texts

Many Christians read their Bible regularly. Everyone has his or her favorite passages, but there are some texts that all Christians know and love.

The Lord's Prayer

Jesus was praying one day when his disciples asked him how they should pray. Jesus replied that they should pray quietly in a room alone. He explained that if a person is not willing to forgive other people, he cannot expect God to forgive him. Jesus gave the disciples the Lord's Prayer. It is used by every Christian. The Lord's Prayer is found in the Gospels of Matthew and Luke.

All Jesus's teaching can be found in the Jewish Bible or in the teaching of the rabbis (Jewish religious teachers). Hillel, a great rabbi who lived just before Jesus, said, "What is horrible to you, do not do to people around you. That is the teaching of the whole of the Jewish scriptures."

"Hands together, eyes closed"—a young Christian girl prays.

"Our Father in heaven, hallowed be your name, your kingdom come, your will be done, on earth as in heaven. Give us today our daily bread. Forgive us the wrong we have done as we have forgiven those who have wronged us. Do not bring us to the test, but save us from evil."

(MATTHEW 6: 9-13)

The two great commandments

Jesus was asked which of all the commandments given by God (see page 13) was the most important. Jesus replied:

"Listen Israel! The Lord your God is the only Lord. Love the Lord your God with all your heart, with all your soul, with all your mind, and with all your strength. The second most important commandment is this: 'Love your neighbor as you love yourself.'" (Mark 12: 29-31)

In these few words, Jesus summed up Jewish teaching. His words were familiar to his listeners because both commandments are taken from the Torah, in the Jewish scriptures.

Love for the world

"For God loved the world so much that He gave His only Son, so that everyone who believes in Him may not die but have eternal life."

(John 3: 16)

These words say simply and clearly what Christians believe about Jesus. Through Jesus, God became human like us. Jesus died so that people could live forever in God's presence. God loved the world so much that He was prepared to see Jesus suffer and die.

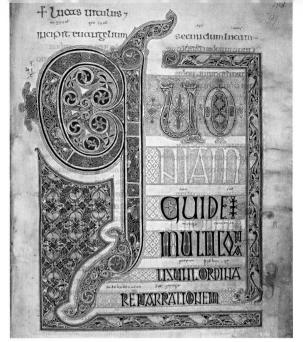

Before the invention of printing, Bibles were handwritten, and many were beautifully decorated. This Bible page dates back to the year 698 C.E.

"There are three things that last forever: faith, hope, and love; but the greatest of these is love."

(1 CORINTHIANS 13: 13)

Paul, writing to a group of Christians at Corinth, in Greece, also put love at the heart of the Christian faith.

"... if I am without love I am a sounding gong or a clanging symbol. ... love is patient, love is kind and envies no one. Love is never boastful nor conceited or rude ... love will never come to an end."

(1 Corinthians 13: 13)

Rites of passage

Christians use their Bibles at special times. They want to show that God is interested and involved in every part of their lives, particularly on special occasions.

Baptism

The baptism of Jesus by John is an important story in the Gospels (see page 16). Christians are baptized when they become followers of Jesus because the Bible tells of Jesus's baptism. The Orthodox, Roman Catholic, and Anglican churches baptize babies to mark the entry of the baby into a new life in the Church. However, churches such as the Baptist Church baptize only adults. Baptists believe that a person needs to be old enough to make his or her own decision to become a Christian.

These African Christians (top) are being baptized in the open air in a stream, while this young baby (bottom) is being baptized in a church.

Marriage

The story of Jesus at the marriage in Cana, in Galilee, is often read at Christian marriage services. Another favorite reading is from one of the letters of Paul, in which he writes about love and its importance (see page 23). When couples get married in church, they commit themselves to each other in the presence of God for the rest of their lives and receive a blessing on their future together.

During wedding ceremonies in Orthodox churches, love crowns are placed on the heads of the bride and groom.

Funerals

Funerals can be very sad times, especially for those who have lost a relative or a close friend. Some Christians, however, see funerals as joyous occasions because they are certain that the dead person has gone to heaven to be with God. During the funeral service, the priest says, "Earth to earth, ashes to ashes, dust to dust." This reminds Christians that after death the body becomes nothing more than dust and that it is not important. It is the soul that is important and lives on with God.

> "Jesus said, 'I am the resurrection and I am life. If a man has faith in me even though he die, he shall come to life; and no one who is alive and has faith shall ever die.'"
>
> (JOHN 11: 25-26)

Orthodox Christian churches do not practice cremation, the burning of the body after death. This is because Orthodox Christians believe that after death, the body should not be destroyed but buried as Jesus was, in a tomb or in the ground. The Roman Catholic Church only accepted cremation in the 1960s.

Church and community

The Bible is used in nearly all church services. In some churches, the service begins with the Bible being carried in procession, before being laid open on a table. In others, the Bible is held aloft in a procession before the Gospel is read. The congregation often stands when the Gospel is read.

Reading from the Bible

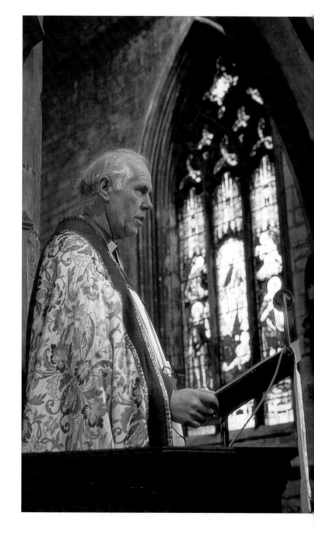

Many church services contain at least two readings from the Bible. There will nearly always be a reading from the Gospels and a reading from the Old Testament or from the Epistles. In Roman Catholic and Anglican churches, the Bible may be carried through the congregation behind people carrying a cross and candles. When the Gospel reading is announced, some readers make the sign of the cross on the Bible. The members of the congregation also make the sign of the cross (touch their forehead, lips, and chest). This shows they wish to keep the words of the Gospel in their minds, on their lips, and in their hearts.

A priest speaks to the congregation during a church service.

"There were indeed many other signs that Jesus performed in the presence of his disciples, which are not recorded in this book. Those here written have been recorded in order that you may hold the faith that Jesus is the Christ, the Son of God, and that through this faith you may possess life by his name."

(JOHN 20: 31)

A Christian mother reads the Bible to her young children.

Private use

Christians worship at home and many read their Bibles every day. They read the Bible to learn more about Jesus. The words of the Bible also help and comfort them at important times in their lives. Christians usually have favorite passages that they read and learn by heart.

Public use

In many Christian countries, the Bible is part of everyday life. For example, in Britain, parliament begins every day with Christian prayers, and in the law courts, witnesses can still swear on a Bible to tell the truth if they wish. Many phrases from the Bible are used in everyday language. Examples include "apple of my eye" and "an eye for an eye, a tooth for a tooth." There are Bibles in most hotel rooms and next to hospital beds. Some church schools give pupils a Bible when they graduate, and some families still have an old family Bible in their homes.

For more than 1,500 years, most Christians were not able to read the Bible. Few people could read, and copies of the Bible were handwritten and very expensive. People learned about the stories in the Bible by going to plays and by looking at stained-glass windows in churches.

Reading and studying the Bible is an important part of being a Christian.

glossary

Abraham He appears in the Old Testament and is regarded as the father of the Jewish people.

Anglican Church Churches across the world that have very close links with the Church of England.

Anoint To place special or blessed oil on a person's head or body.

Apocrypha Books in the Old Testament that are written in Greek, not Hebrew. They are included in the Roman Catholic Bible.

Apostle Someone sent out by Jesus to preach the Gospel.

Baptism A ritual washing with water. Sometimes the water is sprinkled or poured on the person, sometimes the person being baptized is completely submerged in water. It is used in the Christian Church to show the start of a new life in the Church.

Baptist Church A Christian Church that baptizes only adults, rather than children. They believe only mature adults can fully understand what it means to accept Jesus as their savior.

Blasphemy The use of the name of God in a rude or inappropriate way.

Cremation The burning of a body after death.

Crucifixion The Roman method of executing criminals and traitors. They were nailed to a cross to hang until they died.

David A great king of Israel who lived 1,000 years before his descendant, Jesus.

Disciple One who follows Jesus. Originally Jesus chose 12 men (for there were 12 tribes of Israel) to be his closest friends. They were called disciples.

Epistle Comes from the Greek word for "letter." There are several epistles in the New Testament.

Galilee An area in the north of Israel, including the Sea of Galilee.

Gentile A non-Jew.

Gospel Means "good news." In the New Testament, the Gospels are accounts of the life and teaching of Jesus.

Isaiah A leading Israelite prophet whose teaching is in the Old Testament. It was believed he would reappear to announce the coming of the Messiah.

Israelites Descendants of Abraham, the first known Jew. The Israelites were God's chosen people. They escaped from Egypt, led by Moses, to the land God had promised to them, Canaan. Today, Canaan is known as Israel, and the Israelites are more commonly known as Jews.

John the Baptist A relative of Jesus who baptized him at the start of his mission to teach and preach.

Judas The disciple who betrayed Jesus.

Lord's Prayer The prayer given by Jesus to his disciples to teach them how to pray. It is also sometimes known as the "Our Father."

Magi The wise men who visited Jesus at the time of his birth.

Messiah Means "anointed one." It is used by Jews and Christians to describe a person sent by God who will bring a world of peace and justice.

Miracle An event that cannot be explained by the known laws of nature.

Moses The person chosen by God to lead the Israelites out of Egypt more than 3,000 years ago. Moses was also given the Ten Commandments by God on Mount Sinai.

Nazareth The town in Galilee where Jesus was brought up.

New Testament A collection of 27 books which make up the second section of the Christian Bible.

Old Testament A collection of 39 books that Christianity shares with Judaism. These books form the first section of the Christian Bible.

Orthodox Church The Eastern group of Christian churches consisting of national churches such as the Greek Orthodox Church and the Russian Orthodox Church.

Parable A story with hidden meanings. Jesus often used parables to teach.

Passover A festival commemorating the escape of the Israelites from Egypt.

Peter Jesus's chief disciple, to whom he gave authority. The Greek meaning of Peter is "rock."

Prophet A person who speaks God's words and warns of future events.

Psalm A hymn of praise to God, found in the Old Testament.

Rabbi A Jewish religious teacher.

Resurrection Means "raised up." Christians believe that Jesus was raised from the dead by God, and that all people will rise from death on Judgement Day.

Roman Catholic Church The Christian Church that is loyal to the Pope, the Bishop of Rome. It is the largest single Christian Church, with about one million members.

Savior For Christians, the Savior is Jesus, who saves them from their sins and brings eternal life.

Scripture The word often used by Christians to refer to the Bible.

Ten Commandments The commandments given to Moses by God on Mount Sinai. They were rules for the Israelites to live by and are accepted by Christians as part of God's teaching.

Testament Means "promise." Christians believe that the promise of God to the Israelites was fulfilled in Jesus.

Testimony A declaration of truth or fact.

Index